Civil War LEADERS

Wendy Conklin, M.A.

Consultants

Vanessa Ann Gunther, Ph.D.
Department of History
Chapman University

Nicholas Baker, Ed.D.
Supervisor of Curriculum and Instruction
Colonial School District, DE

Katie Blomquist, Ed.S.
Fairfax County Public Schools

Publishing Credits

Rachelle Cracchiolo, M.S.Ed., *Publisher*
Conni Medina, M.A.Ed., *Managing Editor*
Emily R. Smith, M.A.Ed., *Series Developer*
Diana Kenney, M.A.Ed., NBCT, *Content Director*
Courtney Patterson, *Senior Graphic Designer*
Lynette Ordoñez, *Editor*

Image Credits: Cover and p. 1 NativeStock/North Wind Picture Archives; p. 2 Bettmann/Getty Images; p. 4 Bettmann/Getty Images; p. 5 (top) LOC [cw0011000], (bottom left) Granger, NYC, (bottom right) LOC [LC-USZ62-100787]; pp. 6, 8 (bottom), 13 (middle), 14 (bottom), 17 (top right and left), 20-21, 21 (middle), 23 (top), 24, 26 (right) North Wind Picture Archives; pp. 9 (bottom), 10 (top), 18 (bottom), 29 (middle) Granger, NYC; pp. 10-11 Granger, NYC; p. 9 (top) LOC [LC-DIG-pga-02238]; p. 11 (middle) Judson McCranie, used under Creative Commons BY-SA 4.0; p. 12 (left) LOC [LC-DIG-cwpbh-00839], (right) LOC [LC-DIG-ppmsca-19394]; p. 13 (top) LOC [LC-DIG-pga-01851]; p. 14 (top) LOC [LC-USZ62-16405], (center) LOC [LC-DIG-ppmsca-40576]; p. 15 (bottom) LOC [LC-USZ62-102088]; p. 17 (bottom) Historical Documents Co.; p. 18 (top) LOC [LC-USZC2-2687]; p. 19 LOC [LC-USZCN4-273]; p. 20 Samuel Perkins Gilmore prints, University of Kentucky Special Collections Research Center; p. 23 (left) LOC [LC-USZ62-88802]; pp. 24-25 LOC [LC-DIG-pga-01846]; p. 26 (left) LOC [LC-DIG-cwpb-06084], (center) LOC [LC-DIG-cwpbh-00682]; pp. 26-27 (background) LOC [LC-DIG-ppmsca-22570]; p. 27 Bettmann/Getty Images; p. 28 LOC [LC-DIG-pga-06332]; p. 32 and back cover Historical Documents Co.; all other images from iStock and/or Shutterstock.

Library of Congress Cataloging-in-Publication Data

Names: Maloof, Torrey, author.
Title: Abraham Lincoln : addressing a nation / Torrey Maloof.
Description: Huntington Beach, CA : Teacher Created Materials, 2017. |
Includes index.
Identifiers: LCCN 2016034224 (print) | LCCN 2016034285 (ebook) | ISBN
9781493838059 (pbk.) | ISBN 9781480757707 (eBook)
Subjects: LCSH: Lincoln, Abraham, 1809-1865--Juvenile literature. |
Presidents--United States--Biography--Juvenile literature.
Classification: LCC E457.905 .M316 2017 (print) | LCC E457.905 (ebook) | DDC
973.7092 [B] --dc23
LC record available at https://lccn.loc.gov/2016034224

Teacher Created Materials
5301 Oceanus Drive
Huntington Beach, CA 92649-1030
http://www.tcmpub.com

ISBN 978-1-4938-3887-5

Printed in China 51497

Table of Contents

The Union Army

During the Civil War, many men became well-known leaders. They came from all walks of life. These men were thought to be the best minds each side had to offer. Both sides fought heroically for what they believed in.

The **Union** army of the North had many advantages over the **Confederate** army of the South. The North had more men to serve as soldiers. For every two men in the Union army, there was only one man in the Confederate army. The North also had more factories and could produce more **ammunition**. Supplies were easily moved using the railroads in the North. The Northern army had plenty of guns, clothing, and blankets. Their food supply was larger, too.

In spite of all this, the North did have weaknesses. President Abraham Lincoln studied new types of war **strategies** from Washington. He sent orders to the battlefields that the generals had to follow. But, the generals didn't always agree with Lincoln's ideas. Sometimes, they ignored his orders and did what they thought was best. This was frustrating for Lincoln and his generals.

Lincoln had trouble finding a leader that he thought could do a good job. Winfield Scott, George McClellan, John Pope, Ambrose Burnside, Joseph Hooker, and George Meade all tried to lead the Union to victory. But, none of them succeeded. Lincoln struggled throughout the war to find a leader.

BURNSIDE'S SIDEBURNS

General Ambrose Burnside started the trend of growing long whiskers on the sides of men's cheeks. At first, these whiskers were called *burnsides*. Eventually, they became known as *sideburns*.

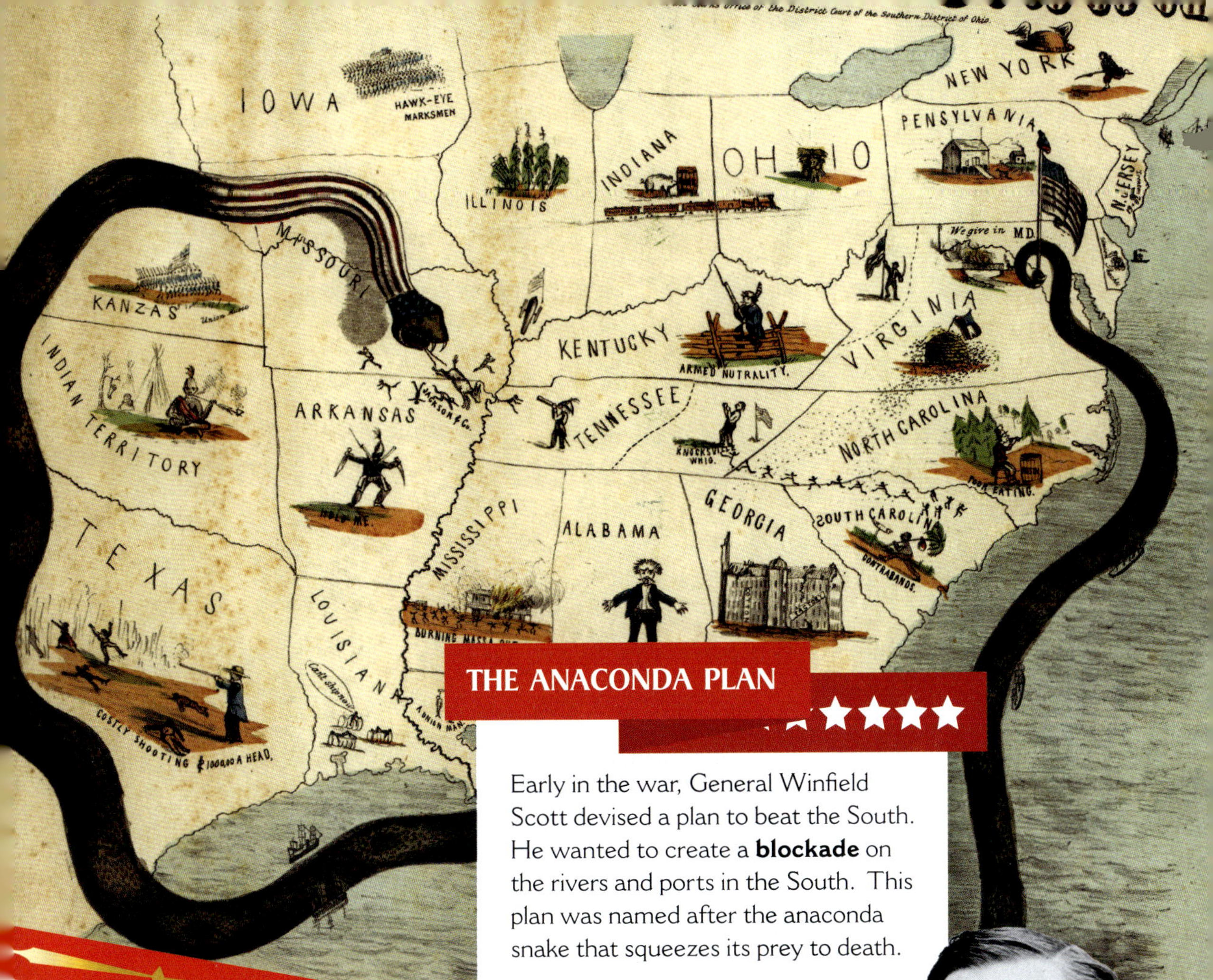

THE ANACONDA PLAN

Early in the war, General Winfield Scott devised a plan to beat the South. He wanted to create a **blockade** on the rivers and ports in the South. This plan was named after the anaconda snake that squeezes its prey to death.

Both the North and the South worked hard to support the war effort.

Winfield Scott

Commander in Chief

In November 1860, Abraham Lincoln was elected as the 16th president. The word *united* did not describe the United States at that time. For a long time, the Southerners and the Northerners had disagreed about how to run the country.

The people in the South wanted the state governments to make the major decisions. For example, Southerners believed each state should decide whether or not it would allow slavery. People in the North believed the federal government should be more involved.

THE POLITICIAN

In his first speech as president, Lincoln said he would not **abolish**, or end, slavery in the slave states. He thought it was more important to keep the country together.

Lincoln spoke out against slavery. He said that enslaved people should have all the rights included in the Declaration of Independence. But, Lincoln's main concern was keeping the nation together. Before he moved into the White House, seven states had **seceded** from the Union. These states formed a new country called the Confederate States of America.

Lincoln had to convince people in the North to go to war. He also had to make sure the North won the war. To do so, he needed good generals, and they were hard to find. Lincoln gave orders and expected the generals to follow them. The generals did not always obey him. Yet, Lincoln was still blamed for each loss. This all changed when Lincoln appointed Ulysses S. Grant.

Ulysses S. Grant

Ulysses S. Grant is one of the most well-known Union leaders. Before the Civil War began, he served in the Mexican-American War and then went into business.

When the Civil War broke out in 1861, Grant quickly joined the North and rose through the ranks. No one expected much of him when he was promoted to general. But, Grant was a determined leader. He knew how to stand his ground and defeat his enemy in battle. He was successful at the Battle of Shiloh. He held Vicksburg under **siege** for almost a year. Grant then took Chattanooga from the South in 1863.

In early 1864, Lincoln named him the commander of the entire Northern army. Just over a year later, Grant met General Robert E. Lee in Appomattox Court House, Virginia, to accept Lee's **surrender**.

Battle of Shiloh

A FOUR-STAR RATING

In 1864, Grant became a lieutenant (loo-TEN-ehnt) general. George Washington had also held that high rank. Two years later, Grant became a four-star general. This was the first time that Congress gave a general that many stars.

Lee surrenders to Grant.

PRESIDENT GRANT

After the war, Grant was elected as the 18th president of the United States. Despite his success in war, Grant faced many challenges while in office. His two terms were filled with **scandals**.

William T. Sherman

William Tecumseh Sherman joined the North in 1861. His ideas about how to win the war impressed Lincoln. So, in 1862, Lincoln promoted Sherman to general. Sherman moved quickly and always kept one goal in mind—to defeat the South. His troops even left supplies behind as they hurried to chase the Confederate army.

Sherman's March to the Sea

Sherman and his soldiers were very successful on the battlefield. But, Sherman was also seen as a ruthless general. His army is best known for its 1864 "March to the Sea." In this march from Atlanta to Savannah, Sherman and his men destroyed much of Georgia. Sherman believed in "total war." He thought the fastest way to win the war was to destroy the South. So that's what they did. Sherman's army dug up parts of the railroad in the South. This prevented the Southern army from receiving their supplies. Sherman's troops burned barns, houses, and fields if the people tried to fight back. Many people in the South said they would never forgive him for this.

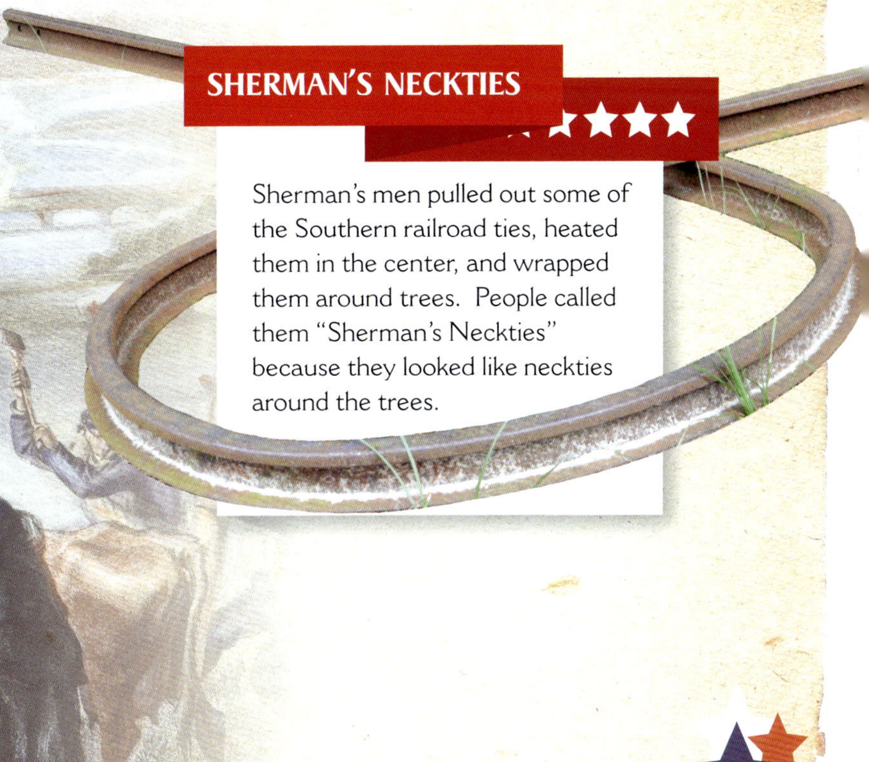

SHERMAN'S NECKTIES

Sherman's men pulled out some of the Southern railroad ties, heated them in the center, and wrapped them around trees. People called them "Sherman's Neckties" because they looked like neckties around the trees.

"Fighting Joe"

When the Civil War began, Joseph Hooker went to Washington, DC. He wanted General Winfield Scott to give him a job as commander. Scott remembered Hooker from school. Hooker was a troublemaker back then. So, Scott ignored Hooker's request. Hooker saw how the South defeated the North at the First Battle of Bull Run. So, he went to the White House and met with President Lincoln. He told Lincoln that if he were in charge at that battle, the North would have won. Lincoln liked his attitude, so he gave Hooker soldiers to command.

Hooker received the nickname "Fighting Joe" after the Battle of Williamsburg due to a printing error in a newspaper. The article was supposed to say, "Fighting—Joe Hooker." But the dash was left out, making it look like a nickname.

Battle of Fredericksburg

General Burnside instructs Hooker in the Battle of Fredericksburg.

"Fighting Joe" went on to the Battles of Antietam and Fredericksburg and fought hard. After so many died at Fredericksburg, Hooker loudly blamed Burnside, the commanding general. Burnside wanted Hooker fired. Instead, Lincoln gave Hooker Burnside's job.

During the Battle of Chancellorsville, Hooker suffered a **concussion** from a canon shot. Some say he lost his nerve after that. He tried to keep fighting Lee's army, but he lost because he kept pulling his men back. Hooker resigned not long after that. Lincoln replaced him with George Meade in 1863.

More Northern Leaders

Many brave men fought for the North. General George McClellan was one of the first commanders of the Northern army. Lincoln chose him to replace the aging Winfield Scott. McClellan's soldiers liked him, but he often froze on the battlefield.

McClellan

General George Meade is probably best known for his command at the Battle of Gettysburg. He led the North to one of its biggest victories. Meade never performed brilliant **maneuvers** in battle. But, he was reliable and knew how to hold his ground.

Reynolds

Just before Gettysburg, Lincoln offered General John Reynolds command of the army. But, Reynolds declined the offer. He died on the first day of the Battle at Gettysburg. His job was to hold off the South until the rest of the Northern army arrived. He succeeded, but he paid with his life.

The 54th Massachusetts **regiment** was made up of black soldiers. They were led by a white commander named Robert Shaw. In 1863, they led a bold **bayonet** charge at Fort Wagner, South Carolina. Many men died and some suffered terrible wounds. Their bravery earned the respect of many people.

CUSTER MAKES HIS DEBUT

George Custer is best known for the Battle of the Little Bighorn in 1876, but he first fought in the Civil War. In fact, his men received a white flag of truce just before Lee surrendered in Appomattox Court House, Virginia.

The 54th Massachusetts regiment attacks Fort Wagner.

General Meade at the Battle of Gettysburg

The Confederacy

Although fighting for a different cause, the South also had many brave leaders. Southerners believed in states' rights. They wanted each state to choose whether to allow slavery. They formed a new country called the Confederate States of America to do just that. It was also known as the Confederacy.

The biggest problem the South faced during the war was its **economy**. The region did not have enough money for all the supplies it would need. It did not have many railroad lines, and most factories were in the North. An army could not survive on only the food from **plantations**. Soldiers needed more resources, such as weapons and ships, to succeed.

LET THE SOUTH GO

Some people in the North wanted to let the South secede. They said the United States did not need the South. Instead, these people wanted to focus on making the United States stronger with just the Northern states.

cotton plantation in the South

Confederate soldiers charge into battle in 1861.

Yet, the South had several advantages. First, it had skilled fighters and excellent generals. Many of these men learned to fight in the Mexican-American War. They were professional soldiers. There were also thousands of farmers who knew how to use their guns. They were used to riding horses and dealing with outdoor life. Southerners fought hard to defend their land.

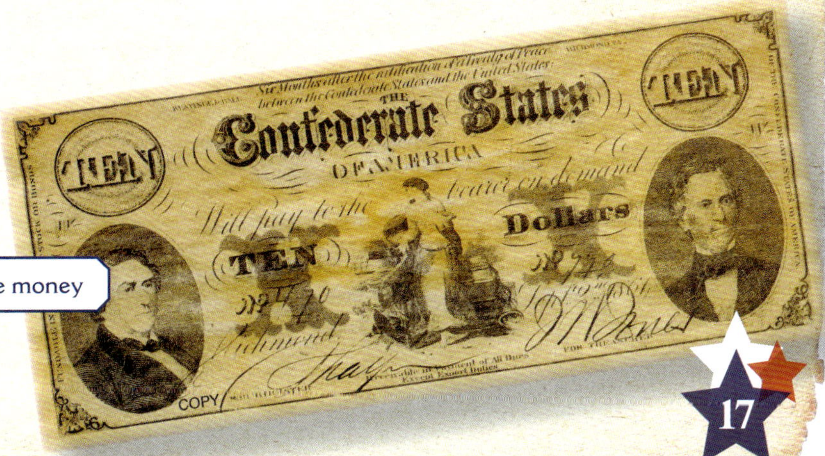

Confederate money

The Other President

Jefferson Davis was very active in government before the Civil War. He served in both houses of Congress and fought in the Mexican-American War. He was a smart man and was made secretary of war in 1853. When the Confederate States of America was formed, Davis seemed like the best choice to lead the new country. He was made its president in 1861.

Jefferson Davis (with a red cloak) and the Confederate generals

But, Davis struggled while in office. He chose his friends as leaders, even when they weren't right for the job. When other generals asked Davis to remove his friends from power, he refused.

Davis also struggled to get his soldiers the supplies they needed. He could not make Southerners pay taxes. Each Southern state acted independently and made its own laws. They had their own money and their own leaders.

So, the South turned to Europe for help. Southerners believed that foreign countries would help the Confederacy because their plantations traded a lot of crops with Europe. But, Europe did not want to get involved in the war. Many European countries did not support slavery. Some did not think the South could win. No one wanted to fight for the losing side. Davis's hopes of European help were crushed.

JAIL TIME

When the war ended, Davis was put in prison for two years. Some people thought Davis was involved in Lincoln's **assassination**. Davis denied that he had anything to do with the president's death.

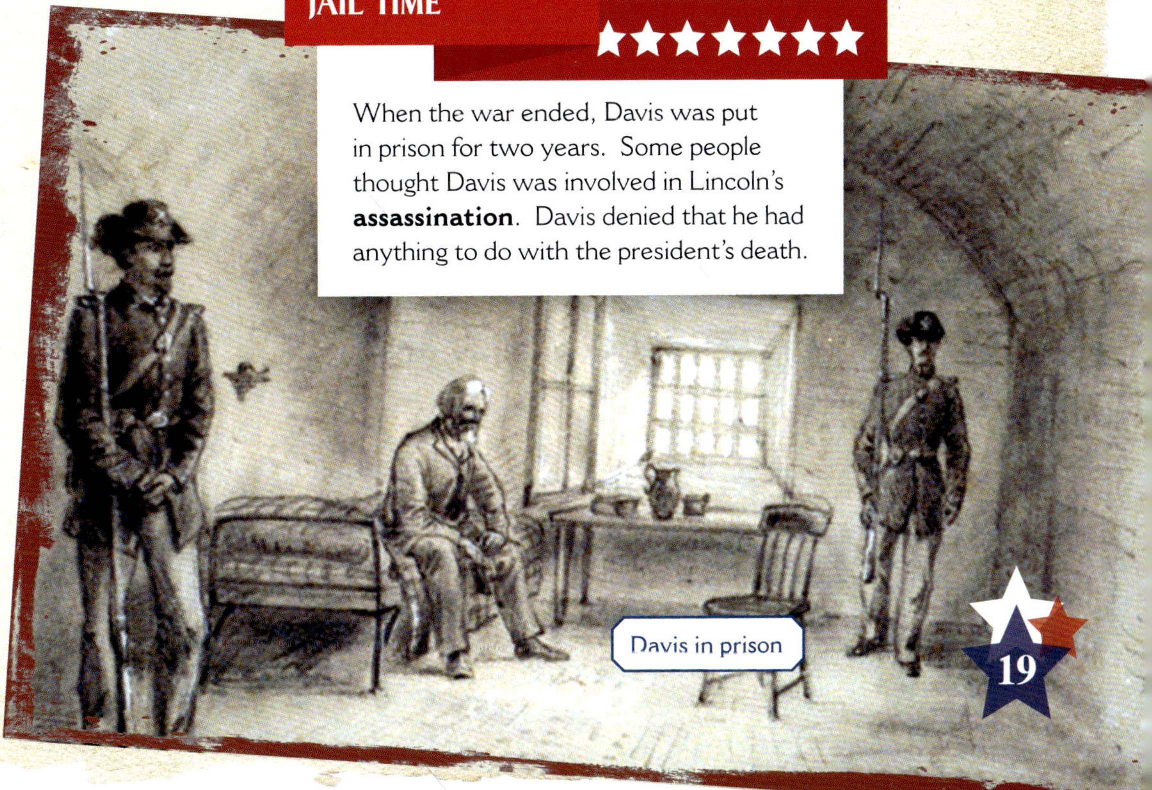

Davis in prison

An Inspiring General

Robert E. Lee is one of the South's most famous generals. Lee was a Virginian. Both the Union and Confederate armies wanted Lee to serve. He truly loved his home state and did not want to fight against it. After thinking it over, he joined the Southern army in 1861.

Lee understood and could plan brilliant military strategies. He inspired his officers and his soldiers to fight and die for the Southern cause.

TRAVELLER THE HORSE

Lee's horse, Traveller, was the most well-known horse in the Civil War. Newspaper reports and photos of Lee mounted on Traveller made the horse a celebrity in both the North and the South.

Battle of Gettysburg

Lee believed in charging at the enemy quickly and with force. Time and time again, his army beat an army more than twice its size. His army seemed unstoppable. But, in July 1863, things began to change. He suffered a terrible defeat at Gettysburg. At the same time, Vicksburg fell in Mississippi. In 1864, Lee's army could not hold off the North at Petersburg and Richmond. Once the Union controlled the Confederate capital of Richmond, Lee knew the war was ending.

When it appeared that he had no other choice, Lee surrendered to General Ulysses S. Grant. The two great men met in a home in Appomattox Court House, Virginia. Lee held his head high, wore his best uniform, and agreed to the surrender.

Lee surrenders at Appomattox Court House in 1865.

LEE'S FAREWELL

In Lee's final speech to his troops, he tried to encourage the defeated army.

> Boys, I have done the best I could for you. Go home now, and if you make as good citizens as you have soldiers, you will do well, and I shall always be proud of you. Good-bye and God bless you all.
>
> – Robert E. Lee

Thomas "Stonewall" Jackson

After serving in the Mexican-American War, Thomas Jackson became a professor. His students did not like him in the classroom, but his men loved him on the battlefield.

During many battles, Jackson led his men to victory against all odds. General Lee called Jackson his "right arm." That meant Lee trusted Jackson and always wanted him nearby.

"Stonewall" Jackson earned his nickname at the First Battle of Bull Run. Jackson's troops were facing heavy fire from the Northern army. One story says that Jackson's men were like a wall that Northern forces could not pass. Another claims that a soldier observed Jackson standing in battle with the resolve of a stone wall. Some people think this was a compliment. Others believe the soldier felt that Jackson should have been marching forward rather than just standing. Regardless of how it happened, soldiers in the North and South began calling him Stonewall Jackson.

Jackson fought hard for the Confederacy. But, at the Battle of Chancellorsville, he was accidentally shot by one of his own men. The wound was so bad that the doctor had to remove Jackson's left arm. Just as it seemed he was getting better, he caught **pneumonia** (nuh-MOH-nyuh) and died. The South mourned their loss.

Jackson leads his troops during the Battle of Chancellorsville.

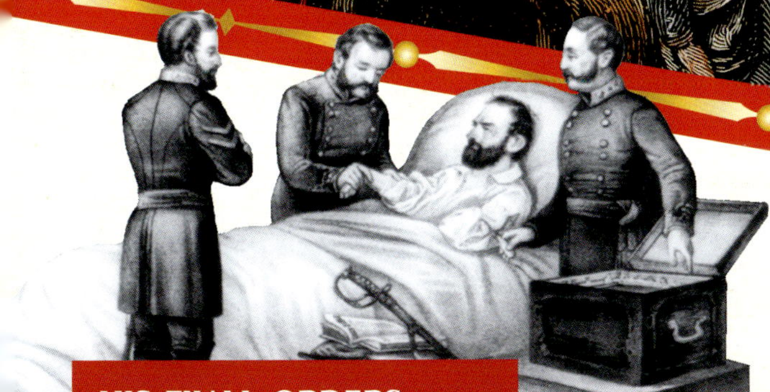

HIS FINAL ORDERS

As Jackson lay dying, he called out these final words, "Prepare for action…Let us cross over the river and rest under the shade of the trees."

statue of Jackson outside the state capital of West Virginia

The One-Legged Commander

John Bell Hood was no stranger to injury in battle. Before the Civil War, an arrow pierced his hand while he was fighting Comanche (kuh-MAN-chee) Indians. Hood calmly pulled out the arrow and continued fighting.

During the Civil War, Hood continued to get injured. While at the Battle of Gettysburg, a shell fragment shattered his left arm. His arm hung limp by his side and was never useful again. Just two months later, he lost his leg to a bullet during the Battle of Chickamauga. His troops raised around $5,000 to buy him a prosthetic leg, but it took a long time to get to him. By then, Hood was anxious to get back into battle. Since there was not enough time to have it properly fitted, Hood's artificial leg was much shorter than his other leg. It was hard for him to walk. But, he asked his troops to strap him to a horse so he could still ride in battle. Hood warned Union troops that he and his men would fight to the death, and they knew he meant it.

Despite his many injuries, Hood continued to rise through the ranks. By the middle of the war, Hood commanded the Texas Brigade and even fought alongside Lee. He was known for aggressively taking on any battle. But as time went on, Hood's luck changed. He and his men found themselves in battles that could not be won. Some blame Hood's defeats on rash decisions. In the end, Lee praised Hood's courage and zeal.

More Southern Leaders

The Confederate army had other great officers. General James Longstreet was a large man. General Lee affectionately called Longstreet, "my old war horse." Longstreet's ideas on war were ahead of his time. He believed in defensive warfare. He spent time trying to convince Lee to dig in rather than charging forward.

In 1862, a Southerner named George Pickett was made a general. Just nine months later, he helped lead a famous charge on the final day of the Battle of Gettysburg. Southern forces were quickly stopped, and nearly half of Pickett's men died that day. The loss haunted Pickett for the rest of his life.

J.E.B. Stuart commanded the Southern **cavalry**. He was respected by his men and quickly rose through the ranks. Time after time, Stuart provided Southern leaders with crucial information about the Northern army. Lee began calling Stuart "the eyes of the army." Before the Battle of Gettysburg, Lee asked Stuart to find out where the Union Army was. But, Stuart didn't arrive until the second day of the battle. Lee openly criticized Stuart for the loss. But many historians now think Stuart was not to blame; there were many other reasons the South lost this battle.

The leaders of the Civil War made the biggest impact on their soldiers. They rallied their men and inspired them to fight for each side's cause. It was their leadership that guided the nation through the long war. As the war came to an end and the nation began to rebuild, the people remembered their leaders. Many are considered war heroes to this day.

Grant

LONGSTREET AND GRANT

Generals Longstreet and Grant were good friends at West Point Military Academy and in the Mexican-American War. Longstreet even attended Grant's wedding. After Grant's death, Longstreet said, "Grant was the truest, as well as the bravest man that ever lived."

Playlist It!

Make a playlist of songs dedicated to some of the leaders in this book. Choose at least five leaders and select a song for each of them. For each song, write a short explanation about why it would be a good fit for the leader. Then, share the playlist with your friends and family. Challenge them to guess which songs are dedicated to which leaders.

Artist:

Song:

Robert E. Lee's song

1:25 3:15

Artist:

Song:

William Sherman's song

1:25 3:15

Artist:

Song:

Abraham Lincoln's song

1:25 3:15

Glossary

abolish—to officially end or stop something

ammunition—bullets and shells that are shot from weapons

assassination—when someone is killed for political reasons

bayonet—a long knife that is attached to the end of a rifle and is often used as a weapon in battle

blockade—an act of war in which ships are used to stop people and supplies from entering or leaving a country

cavalry—an army unit of soldiers that ride horses

concussion—an injury to the brain

Confederate—the group of people who supported the South in the Civil War; comes from the name of the country formed by the states that seceded, the Confederate States of America

economy—the system of buying and selling goods and services

maneuvers—planned movements of soldiers during battles

plantations—large farms that produce crops for money

pneumonia—a serious medical condition that affects the lungs and makes it hard to breathe

regiment—an army unit that can be split into several smaller troops

scandals—behaviors that lead to people thinking you have low moral values

seceded—formally separated from a nation or state

siege—a military blockade of an area that cuts off all contact with the outside world

strategies—careful plans of action to achieve goals

surrender—an agreement to stop fighting because victory is unattainable

Union—term used to describe the United States of America; also the name given to the Northern army during the Civil War

Index

Your Turn!

Confederate Money

Imagine you were put in charge of designing money for the Confederacy. How would it be different from the bill above? How would it be similar? What would each person or symbol represent? Create this new bill and write a short explanation about your design.